MacDougall

by Harry Conroy

Lang**Syne**
PUBLISHING
WRITING *to* REMEMBER

LangSyne

PUBLISHING

WRITING *to* REMEMBER

Vineyard Business Centre,
Pathhead, Midlothian EH37 5XP
Tel: 01875 321 203 Fax: 01875 321 233
E-mail: info@lang-syne.co.uk
www.langsyneshop.co.uk

Design by Dorothy Meikle
Printed by Ricoh Print Scotland
© Lang Syne Publishers Ltd 2009

ISBN 978-1-85217-095-0

MacDougall

SEPT NAMES INCLUDE:

Carmichael
Conacher
Cowan
Dougall
Dowall
Livingston
Livingstone
MacConacher
MacCowan
MacCoul
MacCulloch
MacDowall
MacDowell

MacDulothe
MacEwen
MacEwan
MacEowen
MacOwen
MacHowell
MacKichan
MacLucas
MacLugash
MacLulich
MacNamell
Macoul
Macowl

MacDougall

MOTTO:
Buaidh no bas
(Conquer or Die).

CREST:
"A dexter arm in armour embowed
fessways couped Proper, holding a
cross crosslet fitchée erect Gules".
(A dexter arm holdong a cross).

TERRITORY:
Argyll.

Chapter one:

The origins of the clan system

by Rennie McOwan

The original Scottish clans of the Highlands and the great families of the Lowlands and Borders were gatherings of families, relatives, allies and neighbours for mutual protection against rivals or invaders.

Scotland experienced invasion from the Vikings, the Romans and English armies from the south. The Norman invasion of what is now England also had an influence on land-holding in Scotland. Some of these invaders stayed on and in time became 'Scottish'.

The word clan derives from the Gaelic language term 'clann', meaning children, and it was first used many centuries ago as communities were formed around tribal lands in glens and mountain fastnesses.

The format of clans changed over the centuries, but at its best the chief and his family held the land on behalf of all, like trustees, and the ordinary clansmen and women believed they had a blood relationship with the founder of their clan.

There were two way duties and obligations. An inadequate chief could be deposed and replaced by someone of greater ability.

Clan people had an immense pride in race. Their relationship with the chief was like adult children to a father and they had a real dignity.

The concept of clanship is very old and a more feudal notion of authority gradually crept in.

Pictland, for instance, was divided into seven principalities ruled by feudal leaders who were the strongest and most charismatic leaders of their particular groups.

By the sixth century the 'British' kingdoms of Strathclyde, Lothian and Celtic Dalriada (Argyll) had emerged and Scotland, as one nation, began to take shape in the time of King Kenneth MacAlpin.

Some chiefs claimed descent from

ancient kings which may not have been accurate in every case.

By the twelfth and thirteenth centuries the clans and families were more strongly brought under the central control of Scottish monarchs.

Lands were awarded and administered more and more under royal favour, yet the power of the area clan chiefs was still very great.

The long wars to ensure Scotland's independence against the expansionist ideas of English monarchs extended the influence of some clans and reduced the lands of others.

Those who supported Scotland's greatest king, Robert the Bruce, were awarded the territories of the families who had opposed his claim to the Scottish throne.

In the Scottish Borders country - the notorious Debatable Lands - the great families built up a ferocious reputation for providing warlike men accustomed to raiding into England and occasionally fighting one another.

Chiefs had the power to dispense justice

and to confiscate lands and clan warfare pro-
duced a society where martial virtues - courage,
hardiness, tenacity - were greatly admired.

Gradually the relationship between the
clans and the Crown became strained as Scottish
monarchs became more orientated to life in the
Lowlands and, on occasion, towards England.

The Highland clans spoke a different language, Gaelic, whereas the language of Lowland
Scotland and the court was Scots and in more
modern times, English.

Highlanders dressed differently, had different customs, and their wild mountain land
sometimes seemed almost foreign to people liv-
ing in the Lowlands.

It must be emphasised that Gaelic culture
was very rich and story-telling, poetry, piping, the
clarsach (harp) and other music all flourished and
were greatly respected.

Highland culture was different from
other parts of Scotland but it was not inferior or
less sophisticated.

Central Government, whether in London

"The spirit of the clan means much to thousands of people"

or Edinburgh, sometimes saw the Gaelic clans as a challenge to their authority and some sent expeditions into the Highlands and west to crush the power of the Lords of the Isles.

Nevertheless, when the eighteenth century Jacobite Risings came along the cause of the Stuarts was mainly supported by Highland clans.

The word Jacobite comes from the Latin for James - Jacobus. The Jacobites wanted to restore the exiled Stuarts to the throne of Britain.

The monarchies of Scotland and England became one in 1603 when King James VI of Scotland (1st of England) gained the English throne after Queen Elizabeth died.

The Union of Parliaments of Scotland and England, the Treaty of Union, took place in 1707.

Some Highland clans, of course, and Lowland families opposed the Jacobites and supported the incoming Hanoverians.

After the Jacobite cause finally went down at Culloden in 1746 a kind of ethnic cleansing took place. The power of the chiefs was curtailed. Tartan and the pipes were banned in law.

Many emigrated, some because they wanted to, some because they were evicted by force. In addition, many Highlanders left for the cities of the south to seek work.

Many of the clan lands became home to sheep and deer shooting estates.

But the warlike traditions of the clans and the great Lowland and Border families lived on, with their descendants fighting bravely for freedom in two world wars.

Remember the men from whence you came, says the Gaelic proverb, and to that could be added the role of many heroic women.

The spirit of the clan, of having roots, whether Highland or Lowland, means much to thousands of people.

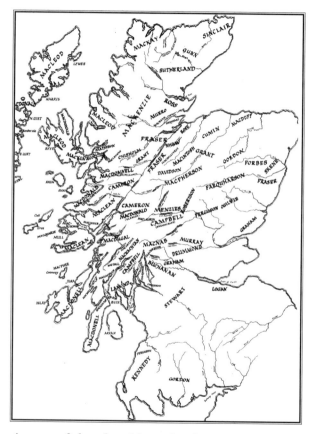

A map of the clans' homelands

Chapter two:

The dark strangers

The MacDougalls are one of the oldest Highland clans, dating back to 1164, when Dougall, eldest son of Somerled, King of the Hebrides and Regulus of Argyll, inherited the central portion of his father's kingdom.

He was given the islands of Mull, Jura, Tiree, Coll, Kerrara and parts of Argyll and Lorne, at a time when the Western Isles were part of Norway and the mainland was ruled by the King of the Scots.

Somerled, who led an uprising against the Norsemen in the mid-twelfth century, knowing that he could not conquer the Viking fleet, proposed to Ragnhilda, the daughter of the Norwegian King, Olaf the Red. At first Olaf refused permission, wanting a more suitable suitor for his daughter but Somerled would not take no for an answer. He ordered his shipwright to swim to Olaf's galley, which was moored at

Ardnamurchan Point and bore holes in the hull.

Carefully positioned near Olaf's galley, Somerled refused to help as the boat began to sink unless Olaf agreed to the marriage. The ruse worked and the couple went on to have two sons, Dougall and Reginald. Dougall went on to found the MacDougall Clan, while Reginald was the founder of Clan Donald.

The MacDougalls were vassals of the Norwegian Kings and the name derives from the words 'mac' which means 'son of' and the gaelic 'dubh gall' which means 'dark stranger' and may have been used to distinguish the darker Danes from the fair-haired Norwegians.

The King of Norway acknowledged Dougall's royal descent, and Dougall styled himself 'King of the South Isles and Lord of Lorne.' Dougall's sons accompanied King Haakon of Norway when he attacked the island of Bute in the Firth of Clyde, following which one of the sons, Duncan, was appointed by Haakon to govern all the islands from the Isle of Man to Lewis.

Duncan, and his son Ewan, built many

castles to defend their extensive dominions, including Dunstaffnage, Dunollie and Duntrune on the mainland and Aros, Cairnburgh, Dunchonnel and Coefinn on the islands.

Ewan, the third chief of the clan, managed to maintain his island holdings from the king of Norway and his mainland titles from the king of Scots, but he found it increasingly hard to remain loyal to both, and in 1263 he was forced to choose allegiance when King Haakon of Norway arrived at Oban with a fleet of more than 200 longships for a planned invasion of the west coast of Scotland.

Ewan declined to join the invasion and because of his blood ties, Haakon left in peace. However Ewan could see that neutrality would ultimately lead to disaster so he decided to attack part of the Norse fleet near Mull.

Haakon and his Viking army were finally defeated at the Battle of Largs and the Western Isles were ceded to Scotland by the Treaty of Perth in 1266.

The Battle of Largs

Chapter three:

Bitter enemies

The MacDougall clan was now at the peak of its power, controlling the entire west coast of Scotland with their huge fleet of galleys, but their Lordship of the Lorne was ambitiously challenged at the end of the thirteenth century by the small clan Duibhne, or Diamid, led by Cailean Mor (Big Colin).

As Cailean Mor gradually forced the MacDougall's boundaries further west, the son of the MacDougall chief, Eion Bachach (Lame John) led the clan, dressed in raven-winged helmets, chainmail and Viking short swords, to war against the Duibhnes.

However MacDougall of Rarey had a bad omen about the impending clash, when he claimed his charm leapt from his sporran and refused to go into battle, leaving the rest of the clan to carry on alone.

When the depleted MacDougalls finally

met Cailean Mor, a bloody clash ensued with tremendous losses on both sides, so that the near-by burn, Ath Dearg (the red ford), turned red with blood. For a time it looked as though the out-numbered MacDougalls would be beaten. However, Cailean Mor was fatally wounded by a MacDougall archer. His followers carried his body away and the battle was over.

The marriage of the fourth chief, Sir Alexander MacDougall, spelled disaster for the clan, as his wife was the sister of John Comyn, Lord of Badenoch, whose son, the Red Comyn, was stabbed to death by Robert the Bruce in the Greyfriars Church in Dumfries in May 1306.

This started a bitter feud between the Bruce and MacDougall families, and although both sides had supported Sir William Wallace and the cause for Scottish independence, they became bitter enemies.

Following his hurried coronation at Scone, Robert the Bruce was forced by the English to retreat to Argyll, where he hoped to meet his Campbell allies. However the

*The quarrel between Comyn
and Robert the Bruce*

MacDougalls surprised the King at Dalrigh, near Tyndrum.

Bruce is said to have escaped only by discarding his cloak on which was found a magnificent example of Celtic jewellery. This later became known as the 'brooch of Lorne', one of the clan's greatest treasures, which remains in possession of the MacDougalls to this day.

It is believed that John of Lorne came close to slaying or capturing the King on a number of occasions. One particularly narrow escape by Robert the Bruce came when John of Lorne pursued Bruce with a bloodhound. Bruce ordered his forces to split again and again but each time the hound followed the party which included the King, until finally, left alone with his foster brother, Bruce was able to throw the hound off his scent by wading down a river.

Two years later when Bruce had firmly established himself on the throne of Scotland, he took his revenge on the MacDougalls when he led 3,000 battle-hardened veterans into Argyll against them.

John of Lorne, fifth chief of the clan and son of Alexander, set an ambush for the king's army at the narrow Pass of Brander, situated between Ben Cruachan and Loch Awe.

Bruce turned the tables on his ambushers by sending a party to ascend the mountain to threaten the MacDougalls from behind while Bruce attacked in front. Despite being outnumbered the MacDougalls held out for some time. However, faced with attack from both directions, they eventually chose to flee.

The MacDougalls were unable to escape the mountain gorge and were slaughtered without mercy by Bruce's men at the Bridge of Awe at a spot still marked by their funeral cairns. Bruce went on to take Argyleshire and the castle of Dunstaffnage, whilst John of Lorne fled to England.

The king formally forfeited the MacDougall lands, much of which passed to the Campbells in recognition of their loyalty.

Chapter four:

New horizons

When Sir John of Lorne arrived in England as a fugitive, King Edward was making preparations for an expedition to Scotland, which ultimately resulted in the Battle of Bannockburn.

John was appointed to the command of the English fleet, and ordered to sail for Scotland, in order to co-operate with the land forces.

Following the defeat of the land troops at Bannockburn, Bruce then directed his efforts to the islands and having arrived at Tarbet it is said he ordered his galleys to the isthmus which connects Kintyre and Knapdale.

The English fleet was surprised and dispersed while John of Lorne was captured and sent to Dumbarton, and later Lochleven, where he was detained for the remainder of King Robert's reign.

The MacDougalls never regained their island possessions, although their fortunes were partly restored when their seventh chief, and son of Sir John of Lorne, Euan MacDougall, married Joan, daughter of Sir Thomas Isaac and Princess Matilda, and a grand-daughter of Robert the Bruce, in 1344. This led to most of their mainland estates being re-granted by a Royal Charter of David II.

These possessions were not to remain in the MacDougall family for long, as Euan died without a son to succeed him around 1375 and most of the MacDougall lands passed to the Campbells when his two daughters and heiresses, Janet and Isabella, married John Stewart of Invermeath, now Invermay, and his brother Robert.

The two brothers had made a pact that John Stewart would obtain the entire Lordship of Lorne while Robert, the younger of the two, secured the family patrimony of Invermeath.

The only part of the Lordship of Lorne which remained in the MacDougall family was Dunolly Castle and its lands, which belonged to the MacDougalls of Dunolly, descended from

Allan MacDougall, Euan's brother. It is from the MacDougalls of Dunolly that the chieftainship of the clan has devolved.

At the beginning of the seventeenth century many members of the MacDougall family migrated to Ireland during the infamous Plantations of Ulster, and many of these later headed to America during the Irish potato famine of 1845-50. As a result the majority of the family members now live in the United States.

Dunolly remained under the control of the MacDougalls until the beginning of the Civil Wars in 1645. The Campbells, whose first fortunes had been founded at the expense of the MacDougalls, had grown in power and in that year the Campbell chief, the Marquess of Argyll, found himself at the head of Government in Scotland as a representative of the party of the Covenant.

For a short time his Royalist rival, the Marquess of Montrose, looked as if he might topple Argyll's leadership, following some victories on the battlefield, including a resounding victory at Inverlochy when Alexander MacDougall led 500 of his clansmen into battle.

However, Montrose's campaign finally ended on September 13th, 1645 when he was defeated at the Battle of Philiphaugh by the Covenanters' army, led by Major-General Sir David Leslie.

Following the Royalist defeat the Marquess of Argyll and General Leslie were employed by Charles I in the reduction of the strongholds held by the dwindling Royalists and in January 1647 they led 6,000 men to Kintyre for the Battle of Rhunahaorine Point, resulting in the deaths of around 80 MacDonalds.

The remaining Royalists, including 49 MacDougalls and 41 Kintyre men, together with a considerable number of MacDonalds under Archibald MacDonald and his son, of Sanda, under the supreme command of John MacDougall of Dunollie, retreated down the peninsula to the fortress of Dunaverty.

When they arrived at Dunaverty they were surrounded by Leslie's troops and, when the

Royalists refused to surrender the house, Leslie attacked the small party defending the one and only supply of water to the fortress.

Without their vital water supply, thirst soon forced the Royalists to surrender the house. More than 300 came out and were immediately slaughtered.

General Leslie was then ordered to attack and destroy the last remaining MacDougall strongholds of Gylen on the island of Kerrera and Dunolly. They were burnt to the ground.

This did not dissuade the MacDougalls from the loyalist cause as they fought with Dundee at Killiecrankie in 1689, and although Alan MacDougall, the 20th clan chief, took an oath of allegiance to King William in 1691, they joined the Jacobite cause in the 1715 under the leadership of Iain Ciar, the 21st chief.

Following the Jacobite failure the Dunolly estate was confiscated and the chief was forced into exile until his death in 1737.

However Dunolly was restored to the family once again in 1745 when Alexander

MacDougall, on the advice of the Duke of Argyll, did not participate in the Jacobite Rising.

It is said that MacDougall met with the Duke of Argyll shortly before Prince Charles

Edward landed at Lochnanuagh. He had in fact been expected to land at Oban, and Stewart of Appin had sent word of his landing to MacDougall.

While waiting for the Duke he saw a horseman arrive at full gallop and shortly afterwards the Duke entered with map in hand and asked MacDougall to point out Lochnanuagh.

Realising that the secret was known, quick-thinking MacDougall seized the opportunity to reveal the details of the landing to the Duke.

The following year the family built Dunollie House, which stands beside the remains of Dunolly Castle. The house was extended in the mid-nineteenth century by the 25th chief, Vice Admiral Sir John MacDougall of MacDougall, and remains the seat of Clan MacDougall today.

The current chief, the 31st, is Morag Morley MacDougall, who inherited the title from her aunt, Coline Helen Elizabeth MacDougall or MacDougall and Dunollie when she died in 1990.

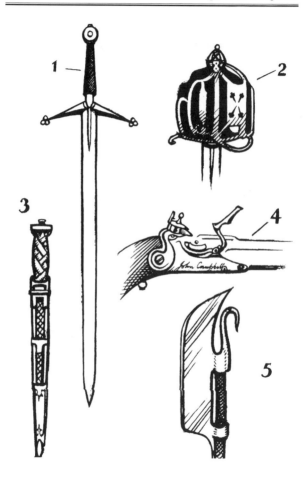

Highland weapons

1)   The claymore or two-handed sword
      (fifteenth or early sixteenth century)

2)   Basket hilt of broadsword
      made in Stirling, 1716

3)   Highland dirk
      (eighteenth century)

4)   Steel pistol *(detail)* made in Doune

5)   Head of Lochaber Axe as carried
      in the '45 and earlier